# mexican

# contents

Mexican is a staple we all love...and it is easier than ever to create delicious Mexican recipes at home. Most supermarkets now stock ingredients such as tortillas, tacos, Mexican flavourings and various salsas, so there's no excuse for not having everyone around for a Mexican night. We even have recipes for sangrita and margaritas!

Pamela Clark

Editorial & Food Director

Australian cup and spoon measurements are metric. A conversion chart appears on page 77.

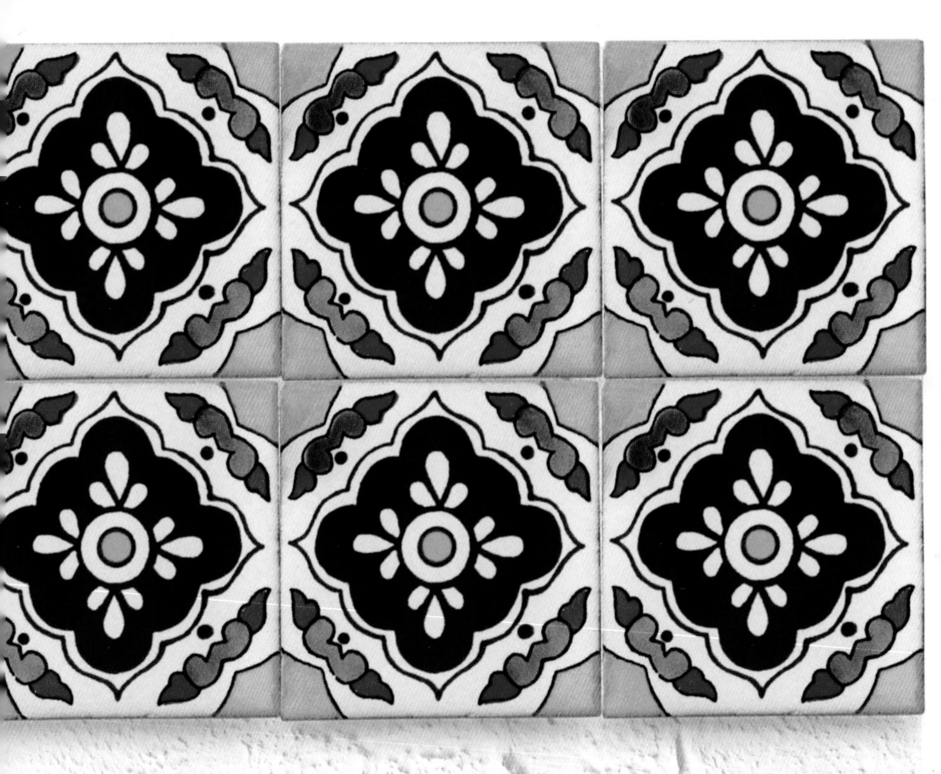

# drinks & starters

Get the evening started with jugs of margaritas and sangritas (not to be confused with the Spanish fruit-based drink, sangria), and plenty of fried tortillas, burritos, empanadas and nachos.

- **2 limes, halved**
- **1 cup ice cubes**
- **45ml (1½ fluid ounces) dark tequila**
- **30ml (1 fluid ounce) blood orange juice**
- **30ml (1 fluid ounce) sugar syrup**

**1** Rub cut side of one lime half around rim of a 260ml (8½-fluid ounce) glass; turn glass upside-down, dip rim into saucer of salt.
**2** Juice limes (you need 30ml of juice).
**3** Shake ice cubes, tequila, juices and sugar syrup in a cocktail shaker; strain into a glass.

**sugar syrup** Stir 1 cup caster (superfine) sugar and 1 cup water in a small pan over low heat until sugar dissolves; bring to the boil, then simmer, without stirring, for 5 minutes. Remove from heat; cool to room temperature. Store in an airtight container in the fridge for up to 1 month.

# blood orange margarita

**serves** 1
**prep time** 5 minutes
**nutritional count per serving** 2.9g total fat (1.3g saturated fat); 836kJ (200 cal); 31.3g carbohydrate; 2.5g protein; 0.1g fibre

**serves** 4
**prep time** 5 minutes
**nutritional count per serving** 0.4g total fat (0g saturated fat); 322kJ (77 cal); 3.1g carbohydrate; 0.4g protein; 0.2g fibre

# sangrita

- ½ cup (125ml) chilled tomato juice
- ⅓ cup (80ml) chilled orange juice
- 2 tablespoons lime juice
- dash Tabasco sauce
- pinch celery salt
- pinch onion powder
- ½ cup (125ml) tequila

**1** Place juices, Tabasco, celery salt and onion powder in a medium jug; mix well. Pour into four 80ml (2½-fluid ounce) tall shot glasses.
**2** Pour tequila into four shot glasses; serve sangrita alongside tequila shooters.

# shredded pork and bean soup

- **1 large carrot (180g), chopped coarsely**
- **1 trimmed celery stalk (100g), chopped coarsely**
- **5 cloves garlic, unpeeled, bruised**
- **3 sprigs fresh oregano**
- **6 black peppercorns**
- **1 dried bay leaf**
- **1kg (2-pound) piece pork neck**
- **2 litres (8 cups) chicken stock**
- **2 litres (8 cups) water**
- **1 tablespoon olive oil**
- **1 large red onion (300g), chopped coarsely**
- **1 medium red capsicum (bell pepper) (200g), chopped coarsely**
- **1 medium yellow capsicum (bell pepper) (200g), chopped coarsely**
- **2 fresh long red chillies, sliced thinly**
- **2 cloves garlic, crushed**
- **810g (1½ pounds) canned crushed tomatoes**
- **1 teaspoon ground cumin**
- **2 tablespoons coarsely chopped fresh oregano**
- **420g (13½ ounces) canned kidney beans, drained, rinsed**

**1** Place carrot, celery, bruised garlic, oregano sprigs, peppercorns, bay leaf, pork, stock and the water in a large saucepan; bring to the boil. Reduce heat; simmer, covered, 1 hour. Uncover; simmer for 1 hour.

**2** Transfer pork to a medium bowl; shred pork coarsely. Strain broth through a muslin-lined sieve or colander into a large heatproof bowl; discard solids.

**3** Heat oil in the same cleaned pan; cook onion, capsicums, chilli and crushed garlic, stirring, over medium heat, for about 5 minutes or until vegetables soften.

**4** Return pork and broth to pan with tomatoes, cumin and chopped oregano; bring to the boil. Reduce heat; simmer, covered, 15 minutes. Add beans; simmer, covered, until soup is hot. Season to taste.

**serves** 6
**prep + cook time** 3 hours
**nutritional count per serving** 7.4g total fat (1.6g saturated fat); 1490kJ (356 cal); 20.8g carbohydrate; 46.5g protein; 9.1g fibre

BEST BEFORE
032 14:02

# chipotle beef tostaditas

**These delicious little bites are fried tortillas with a beef topping.**

- **2 chipotle chillies**
- **½ cup (125ml) boiling water**
- **12 x 17cm (6¾-inch) round white corn tortillas**
- **vegetable oil, for deep-frying**
- **1 tablespoon vegetable oil, extra**
- **1 small brown onion (80g), sliced thinly**
- **1 clove garlic, crushed**
- **280g (9 ounces) minced (ground) beef**
- **1 tablespoon tomato paste**
- **1 cup (250ml) beer**
- **¼ cup coarsely chopped fresh coriander (cilantro)**
- **½ cup (120g) sour cream**

**makes** 36
**prep + cook time**
55 minutes (+ standing)
**nutritional count per piece**
3.2g total fat
(1.3g saturated fat); 238kJ
(57 cal); 4.3g carbohydrate;
2.4g protein; 0.6g fibre

**1** Cover chillies with the boiling water in a small heatproof bowl; stand 20 minutes.
**2** Meanwhile, cut three 7cm (2¾-inch) rounds from each tortilla. Heat oil in a medium frying pan over high heat; deep-fry rounds, in batches, until browned lightly. Drain on kitchen paper.
**3** Drain chillies over a small bowl; reserve liquid. Discard stems from chillies. Blend chillies and reserved liquid until smooth.
**4** Heat extra oil in a medium frying pan; cook onion, stirring, until softened. Add garlic and beef; cook, stirring, until beef is changed in colour. Stir in paste, beer and chilli puree; bring to the boil. Reduce heat; simmer, uncovered, for about 15 minutes or until liquid is almost evaporated. Stir in coriander; season.
**5** To serve, top each tortilla crisp with a rounded teaspoon of the chipotle beef then top with ½ teaspoon of the sour cream.

# margarita

- **2 limes, halved**
- **1 cup ice cubes**
- **45ml (1½ fluid ounces) dark tequila**
- **30ml (1 fluid ounce) orange-flavoured liqueur**
- **30ml (1 fluid ounce) sugar syrup (see recipe, page 6)**

**1** Rub cut side of one lime half around rim of 150ml (4½-fluid ounce) margarita glass; turn glass upside-down and dip wet rim into saucer of salt.

**2** Juice limes (you need 30ml/1 fluid ounce of juice).

**3** Place ice cubes, tequila, liqueur, juice and syrup in cocktail shaker; shake vigorously. Strain into glass. Garnish with shredded lime rind made using a zester.

**serves** 1
**prep time** 5 minutes
**nutritional count per serving** 0.2g total fat (0g saturated fat); 1216kJ (291 cal); 31.4g carbohydrate; 0.3g protein; 0.1g fibre

**serves** 1
**prep time** 5 minutes
**nutritional count per serving** 0.2g total fat (0g saturated fat); 1216kJ (291 cal); 31.4g carbohydrate; 0.3g protein; 0.1g fibre

# frozen margarita

- **2 limes, halved**
- **1½ cups ice cubes**
- **45ml (1½ fluid ounces) dark tequila**
- **30ml (1 fluid ounce) orange-flavoured liqueur**
- **30ml (1 fluid ounce) sugar syrup (see recipe, page 6)**

**1** Rub cut side of one lime half around rim of 150ml (4½-fluid ounce) margarita glass; turn glass upside-down and dip wet rim into saucer of salt.
**2** Juice limes (you need 30ml/1 fluid ounce of juice).
**3** Blend ingredients until smooth. Pour into glass; garnish with fresh mint leaves and lime slices.

# shredded pork chimichanga

**Nothing goes better with a jug of margarita or a cold Mexican beer than one of these deep-fried burritos.**

- **500g (1 pound) diced pork**
- **3 cloves garlic**
- **2 black peppercorns**
- **1 teaspoon ground cumin**
- **3 cups (750ml) water**
- **½ cup coarsely chopped fresh coriander (cilantro)**
- **1 small red onion (100g), chopped finely**
- **2 fresh green jalapeño chillies, seeded, chopped finely**
- **8 x 20cm (8-inch) flour tortillas**
- **vegetable oil, for deep-frying**

**makes** 8
**prep + cook time** 2 hours (+ cooling)
**nutritional count per serving** 13.3g total fat (2.9g saturated fat); 1087kJ (260 cal); 18.2g carbohydrate; 16.4g protein; 1.3g fibre

**1** Place pork, garlic, peppercorns, cumin and the water in a large saucepan; bring to the boil. Reduce heat; simmer, covered, about 1 hour or until pork is tender. Cool.
**2** Drain liquid from pork; discard peppercorns and liquid. Shred pork and garlic, using two forks. Combine pork mixture with coriander, onion and chilli in a large bowl; season to taste.
**3** Heat tortillas following directions on the packet. Divide pork mixture evenly between tortillas; roll up firmly, secure with toothpick at each end.
**4** Heat oil in a large frying pan over high heat; deep-fry tortilla rolls, in batches, until browned lightly. Drain on kitchen paper. Remove toothpicks.
**5** Cut each chimichanga in half; serve with guacamole (see recipe on page 70).

# pork, olive and egg empanadas

**An empanada is a stuffed pastry. You need 2 hard-boiled eggs for this recipe.**

- **1 tablespoon olive oil**
- **1 medium brown onion (150g), chopped finely**
- **½ teaspoon each ground cumin, cinnamon and smoked paprika**
- **¼ teaspoon each ground nutmeg and cloves**
- **375g (12 ounces) minced (ground) pork**
- **2 hard-boiled eggs, grated coarsely**
- **⅓ cup (40g) pitted black olives, chopped finely**
- **6 sheets shortcrust pastry**
- **1 egg, beaten lightly**
- **lemon wedges, to serve**

**1** Heat oil in a large frying pan over medium heat; cook onion, stirring, about 5 minutes or until soft. Add spices and pork; cook, stirring, over high heat, until browned. Cool.
**2** Stir hard-boiled eggs and olives into pork mixture; season to taste.
**3** Preheat oven to 200°C/400°F. Oil two oven trays.
**4** To make empanadas, cut 24 x 12cm (5-inch) rounds from pastry. Drop heaped tablespoons of filling onto rounds; brush edges with beaten egg. Fold rounds in half to enclose filling; pinch edges to seal.
**5** Place empanadas on oven trays with the sealed edge upright; brush top with beaten egg.
**6** Bake empanadas about 25 minutes or until browned lightly. Serve with lemon wedges.

**makes** 24
**prep + cook time** 1 hour (+ cooling)
**nutritional count per empanada** 14g total fat (6.7g saturated fat); 961kJ (230 cal); 19.2g carbohydrate; 6.7g protein; 0.9g fibre

- 2 teaspoons vegetable oil
- ½ small green capsicum (bell pepper) (75g), chopped finely
- ½ small brown onion (40g), chopped finely
- 1 tablespoon pickled sliced jalapeño chillies, drained, chopped finely
- 1 clove garlic, crushed
- 200g (6½ ounces) canned chopped tomatoes
- 250g (8 ounces) cream cheese, softened

**1** Heat oil in a medium saucepan over medium heat; cook capsicum, onion, chilli and garlic, stirring, about 5 minutes or until onion softens. Add undrained tomatoes; cook, stirring, 2 minutes.

**2** Add cream cheese; whisk until combined and dip is smooth. Season to taste.

**3** Serve cheese dip hot, accompanied with corn chips, if you like.

# chile con queso

**makes** 2 cups
**prep + cook time** 20 minutes
**nutritional count per tablespoon dip** 3.9g total fat (2.3g saturated fat); 171kJ (41 cal); 0.7g carbohydrate; 1g protein; 0.2g fibre

**serves** 4
**prep time** 15 minutes (+ refrigeration)
**nutritional count per serving** 18.5g total fat (3.4g saturated fat); 1685kJ (403 cal); 4g carbohydrate; 52.5g protein; 1.9g fibre

# ceviche

- **1kg (2 pounds) skinless redfish fillets**
- **1½ cups (375ml) lime juice**
- **¼ cup (40g) pickled sliced jalapeño chillies, drained**
- **¼ cup (60ml) olive oil**
- **250g (8 ounces) mixed baby tomatoes, chopped coarsely**
- **¼ cup finely chopped fresh coriander (cilantro)**
- **1 small red onion (100g), sliced thinly**
- **1 clove garlic, crushed**

**1** Discard any skin or bones from fish; cut fish into 2.5cm (1-inch) pieces.
**2** Combine fish and juice in large glass bowl. Cover; refrigerate overnight.
**3** Drain fish; discard juice. Return fish to bowl, add remaining ingredients; toss gently to combine. Cover; refrigerate 1 hour. Season to taste.

**tip** You need about 10 limes for this recipe.

# bean nachos

- 800g (1½ pounds) canned kidney beans, rinsed, drained
- ⅓ cup (85g) chunky tomato salsa
- ⅓ cup finely chopped fresh coriander (cilantro)
- 200g (7 ounces) packet corn chips
- 1½ cups (180g) coarsely grated cheddar
- 2 cups (120g) finely shredded iceberg lettuce
- 1 small tomato (90g), chopped coarsely
- ½ small avocado (100g), chopped coarsely
- 2 tablespoons lime juice

**1** Preheat oven to 220°C/425°F.
**2** Combine half the beans with salsa in a medium bowl; mash until chunky. Stir in remaining beans and coriander.
**3** Spread half the chips in a medium shallow baking dish; top with half the cheese and half the bean mixture. Top with remaining chips, cheese then remaining bean mixture. Bake 10 minutes.
**4** Place lettuce, tomato and avocado in a medium bowl with juice; toss gently to combine. Season to taste.
**5** Serve nachos topped with salad.

**serves** 6
**prep + cook time** 20 minutes
**nutritional count per serving** 24.5g total fat (11.6g saturated fat); 1856kJ (444 cal); 33.7g carbohydrate; 17.3g protein; 10.8g fibre

**tips** This is our version of huevos rancheros, or ranch-style eggs, which traditionally is made with fried eggs and beans. For extra bite, serve with Tabasco, a fiery sauce made from hot red chillies.

# scrambled eggs with fresh tomato salsa

- **3 cured chorizo sausages (500g), sliced thickly**
- **8 eggs**
- **½ cup (125ml) pouring cream**
- **20g (¾ ounce) butter**
- **4 x 15cm (6-inch) flour tortillas**
- **1 cup (120g) coarsely grated cheddar**

## fresh tomato salsa

- **2 small tomatoes (180g), chopped finely**
- **½ small red onion (50g), chopped finely**
- **1 tablespoon red wine vinegar**
- **1 tablespoon olive oil**
- **¼ cup coarsely chopped fresh coriander (cilantro)**

**1** Preheat oven to 160°C/325°F.

**2** Make fresh tomato salsa.

**3** Cook chorizo in a medium frying pan over medium-high heat until well browned. Drain on kitchen paper; cover to keep warm. Wipe pan clean.

**4** Whisk eggs and cream in a medium bowl. Melt butter in same frying pan; cook egg mixture over low heat, stirring gently, until creamy.

**5** Meanwhile, place tortillas on an oven tray, sprinkle with cheese; warm in oven until cheese is melted.

**6** Divide tortillas between serving plates; top with egg, chorizo and salsa.

**fresh tomato salsa** Combine tomato, onion, vinegar and oil in small bowl. Cover; stand for 15 minutes. Stir in coriander just before serving; season to taste.

**serves** 4
**prep + cook time** 20 minutes
**nutritional count per serving** 81.7g total fat (35.8g saturated fat); 4126kJ (987 cal); 16.2g carbohydrate; 48.2g protein; 1.9g fibre

# mains

One thing that the Mexicans do well is chilli (or chile), and it is a staple in most of the recipes in this chapter. Remove the seeds and membranes from the chilli to reduce the amount of heat.

# fish burritos

- 1 cup coarsely chopped fresh coriander (cilantro)
- 2 teaspoons finely chopped coriander (cilantro) root and stem mixture
- 1 fresh long red chilli, chopped coarsely
- 1 clove garlic, quartered
- 1½ teaspoons sweet paprika
- 1 teaspoon ground cumin
- ⅓ cup (80ml) olive oil
- 800g (1½ ounces) small white fish fillets, halved
- 8 x 20cm (8-inch) flour tortillas
- 1 baby cos (romaine) lettuce (180g), leaves separated
- 1 lebanese cucumber (130g), sliced thinly

## lime buttermilk dressing

- ¼ cup (60ml) buttermilk
- 1 teaspoon finely grated lime rind
- 2 teaspoons lime juice

**1** Blend or process the chopped coriander and the root and stem mixture with chilli, garlic, spices and ¼ cup of the oil until smooth. Combine the coriander mixture and fish in a large bowl. Cover; refrigerate 30 minutes.

**2** Meanwhile, make lime buttermilk dressing.

**3** Heat remaining oil in a large frying pan over medium-high heat; cook fish, in batches, until browned both sides and cooked through. Cover to keep warm.

**4** Meanwhile, heat tortillas according to directions on packet.

**5** Divide lettuce, cucumber, fish and dressing between tortillas; wrap firmly to enclose filling.

**lime buttermilk dressing** Combine ingredients in a small jug; season to taste.

**makes** 8
**prep + cook time** 30 minutes (+ refrigeration)
**nutritional count per burrito** 14g total fat (2.5g saturated fat); 1267kJ (303 cal); 19g carbohydrate; 24.3g protein; 2g fibre

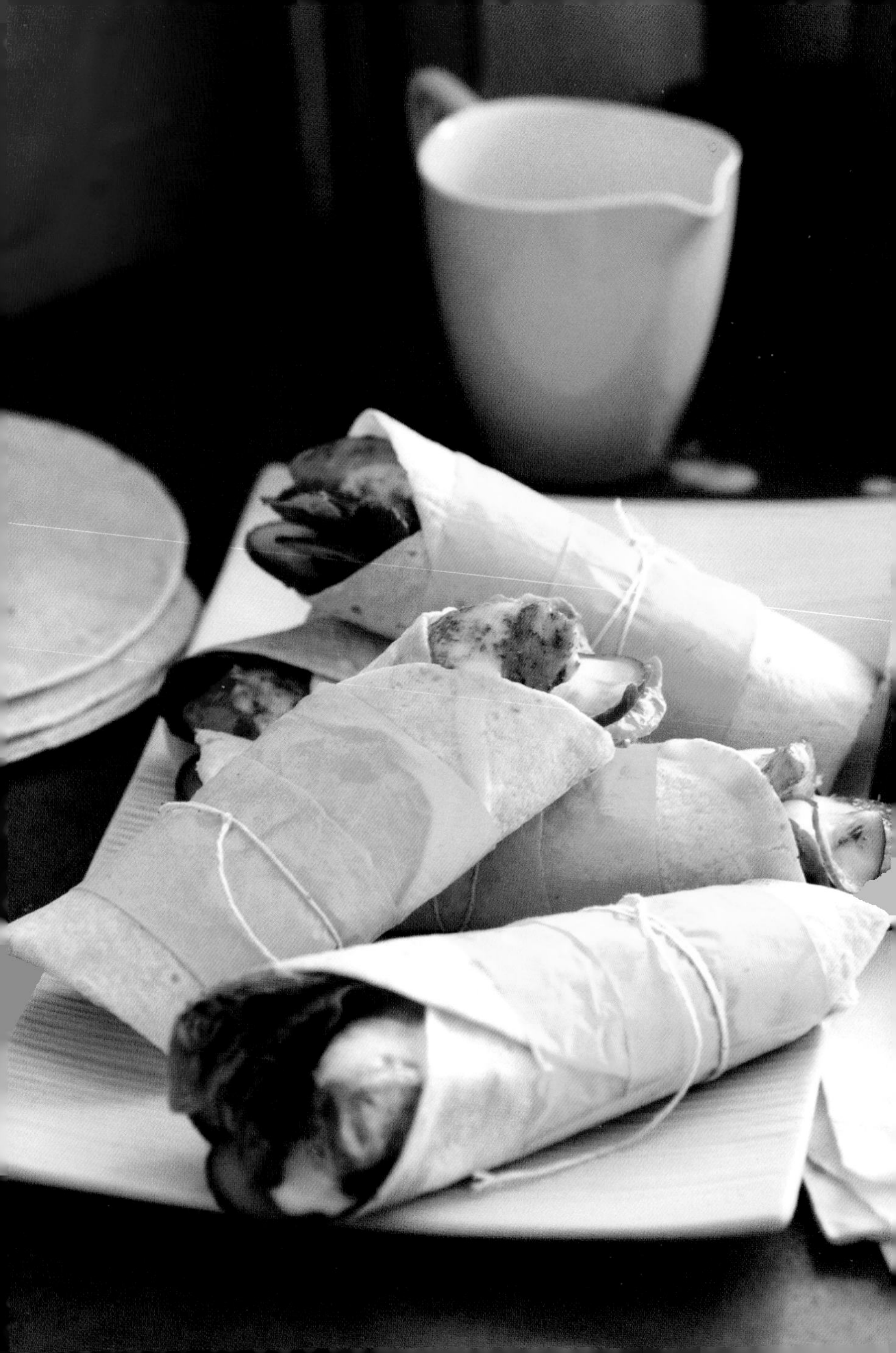

**tip** Soak unshucked corn cobs in a pan of cold water for an hour or so. Pull back each cob's husk without removing it then remove the silk. Brush melted butter over the kernels then re-cover the cob with the husk. Put corn directly on a hot barbecue grill for about 10 minutes, turning once. The result is delicious.

# char-grilled scallops with corn salsa

- 36 scallops (900g), roe removed
- 2 cloves garlic, crushed
- 2 tablespoons lime juice
- 1 tablespoon olive oil
- 2 corn cobs (800g), trimmed
- 200g (6½ ounces) grape tomatoes, halved
- 1 large avocado (320g), chopped coarsely
- 1 medium red onion (170g), chopped finely
- 1 medium green capsicum (bell pepper) (200g), chopped finely
- 2 fresh small red thai (serrano) chillies, chopped finely
- ¼ cup coarsely chopped fresh coriander (cilantro)
- 8 x 15cm (6-inch) white corn tortillas
- lime wedges, to serve

## lime dressing

- ¼ cup (60ml) lime juice
- ½ teaspoon ground cumin
- 2 teaspoons olive oil

**1** Combine scallops, garlic, juice and oil in a large bowl. Cover; refrigerate 3 hours or overnight.

**2** Make lime dressing.

**3** Cook corn on a heated oiled grill plate (or grill or barbecue) until browned lightly and just tender. When cool enough to handle, cut kernels from cobs. Combine corn kernels in a large bowl with tomato, avocado, onion, capsicum, chilli, coriander and dressing; season to taste.

**4** Cook drained scallops, in batches, on same heated grill plate until browned lightly and cooked as desired. Remove from heat; cover to keep warm.

**5** Using tongs, place tortillas, one at a time, briefly, on same grill plate to lightly brown both sides (work quickly as the tortillas will toughen if overcooked). Wrap tortillas in a tea towel to keep warm.

**6** Serve scallops with corn salsa, tortillas and lime wedges.

**lime dressing** Place ingredients in screw-top jar; shake well.

**serves** 4
**prep + cook time** 45 minutes (+ refrigeration)
**nutritional count per serving** 24.1g total fat (4.4g saturated fat); 2416kJ (578 cal); 50.6g carbohydrate; 37.8g protein; 12.2g fibre

# beef burritos

- **1 tablespoon olive oil**
- **1 medium brown onion (150g), chopped finely**
- **1 clove garlic, crushed**
- **1 teaspoon ground cumin**
- **¼ teaspoon chilli powder**
- **500g (1 pound) minced (ground) beef**
- **400g (12½ ounces) canned crushed tomatoes**
- **½ cup (125ml) water**
- **400g (12½ ounces) canned kidney beans, rinsed, drained**
- **4 x 20cm (8-inch) flour tortillas**
- **1 cup (120g) coarsely grated cheddar**
- **1 teaspoon hot paprika**
- **¾ cup (180g) sour cream**
- **¼ cup fresh coriander (cilantro) leaves**

**1** Heat oil in a medium frying pan over high heat; add onion, garlic, cumin and chilli powder; cook, stirring, about 3 minutes or until onion softens. Add beef; cook, stirring, until browned. Stir in tomatoes, the water and beans; simmer, uncovered, about 15 minutes or until mixture thickens. Remove from heat; season to taste.

**2** Preheat oven to 200°C/400°F.

**3** Divide warm beef filling between tortillas, roll to enclose filling; secure with toothpicks.

**4** Place filled tortillas on oiled oven tray; sprinkle with cheese and paprika.

**5** Bake burritos about 10 minutes or until heated through. Remove toothpicks; serve burritos topped with sour cream, coriander and, if you like, guacamole (see page 70).

**makes** 4
**prep + cook time** 55 minutes
**nutritional count per burrito** 45g total fat (24g saturated fat); 3022kJ (723 cal); 34.1g carbohydrate; 42.4g protein; 7.3g fibre

**serves** 6
**prep + cook time** 1½ hours
**nutritional count per serving**
51.9g total fat (15.3g saturated fat); 3294kJ (788 cal); 20.1g carbohydrate; 52.8g protein; 3.3g fibre

# chicken mole

- 6 x 500g (1-pound) small chickens
- ⅓ cup (50g) plain (all-purpose) flour
- ¼ cup (60ml) olive oil
- 1 medium brown onion (150g), chopped finely
- 2 fresh long red chillies, sliced thinly
- 2 cloves garlic, crushed
- 1 cinnamon stick
- ½ teaspoon ground nutmeg
- ¼ teaspoon ground cloves
- 800g (1½ pounds) canned crushed tomatoes
- 1 large red capsicum (bell pepper) (350g), sliced thinly
- 1 cup (250ml) dry white wine
- 60g (2 ounces) dark (semi-sweet) chocolate, chopped finely
- ⅓ cup coarsely chopped fresh flat-leaf parsley

**1** Rinse chickens under cold water; pat dry with kitchen paper. Using kitchen scissors, cut along both sides of chickens' backbones; discard backbones. Halve chickens along the breastbones then cut each half into two pieces.

**2** Coat chicken in flour; shake off excess. Heat oil in a large frying pan over high heat; cook chicken, in batches, until browned. Drain on kitchen paper.

**3** Cook onion, chilli and garlic in same pan, stirring, over medium heat, about 5 minutes or until onion softens. Add spices to pan; cook, stirring, for 30 seconds or until fragrant.

**4** Return chicken to pan with tomatoes, capsicum and wine; simmer, covered, 20 minutes. Uncover; simmer about 20 minutes or until chicken is tender and sauce thickens slightly.

**5** Add chocolate; cook, stirring, until smooth. Season to taste. Discard cinnamon stick. Serve chicken with sauce; sprinkle with parsley.

**serving suggestion**

Serve with steamed green beans and rice or a green salad, and crusty bread to mop up the juices.

# chicken in pumpkin seed and tomatillo sauce

- **2 medium tomatoes (300g), quartered**
- **1 medium brown onion (150g), quartered**
- **2 tablespoons olive oil**
- **6 chicken thigh cutlets (1.2kg)**
- **6 chicken drumsticks (900g)**
- **1½ cups (375ml) chicken stock**
- **1 cup (200g) pumpkin seed kernels (pepitas), roasted**
- **2 tablespoons pickled sliced jalapeño chillies, drained**
- **½ cup (125g) drained chopped tomatillos**
- **2 cloves garlic, quartered**
- **½ cup firmly packed fresh coriander (cilantro) leaves**
- **⅓ cup coarsely chopped fresh chives**
- **½ teaspoon ground cumin**

**1** Preheat oven to 200°C/400°F.

**2** Place tomato and onion on an oiled oven tray; drizzle with half the oil. Roast, uncovered, about 25 minutes or until vegetables soften. Cool.

**3** Meanwhile, place chicken in a large saucepan with stock; bring to the boil. Reduce heat; simmer, covered, about 20 minutes or until chicken is just cooked through. Remove chicken from pan; reserve 1¼ cups of stock.

**4** Blend or process pumpkin seed kernels into a fine powder; sift powder through a fine sieve. Blend or process pumpkin seed powder with tomato and onion mixture, chilli, tomatillos, garlic, coriander, chives and cumin until smooth.

**5** Heat remaining oil in same cleaned pan; cook chicken, in batches, until browned. Remove from pan. Add pumpkin seed mixture to pan; cook, stirring, 3 minutes. Add reserved stock; simmer, uncovered, 2 minutes. Return chicken to pan; simmer, uncovered, until chicken is heated through. Season to taste.

**serving suggestion**
Serve with steamed rice, lime wedges and fresh coriander leaves (cilantro).

**serves** 6
**prep + cook time** 1 hour
**nutritional count per serving** 52g total fat (13g saturated fat); 2959kJ (708 cal); 8.6g carbohydrate; 50.1g protein; 5g fibre

**tip** Tomatillos belong to the same family as the tomato (nightshade), but have a papery outer skin and a tart flavour. They're most often green in colour, although they may also be yellow, red and purplish. Also known as 'mexican green tomato', or 'tomato verde'.

**tip** Meatballs and sauce can be made a day ahead; cover, separately, and refrigerate.

# albóndigas

Meaning 'meatballs', this can be made into a child-friendly (and non-Mexican) alternative: just delete the chilli and serve the meatballs with pasta.

- 2 tablespoons vegetable oil
- 1 medium brown onion (150g), chopped finely
- 1 clove garlic, crushed
- 1 teaspoon each ground cumin and coriander
- ½ teaspoon chilli powder
- 750g (1½ pounds) minced (ground) beef
- 800g (1½ pounds) canned crushed tomatoes
- 410g (13 ounces) canned mexican-style beans
- ⅓ cup (80g) sour cream
- ⅓ cup loosely packed fresh coriander leaves (cilantro)

**serves** 4
**prep + cook time** 50 minutes
**nutritional count per serving** 32.2g total fat (13.4g saturated fat); 2349kJ (562 cal); 20.4g carbohydrate; 44.6g protein; 7.8g fibre

**1** Heat half the oil in a large frying pan over medium heat; cook onion, garlic and spices, stirring, about 5 minutes or until onion softens. Cool.
**2** Combine beef with onion mixture in a medium bowl; season. Using hands, roll level tablespoons of mixture into balls.
**3** Heat remaining oil in the same pan over high heat; cook meatballs, in batches, until browned all over. Remove from pan.
**4** Add tomato and beans to same pan; bring to the boil. Reduce heat; simmer, uncovered, for about 5 minutes or until mixture thickens slightly. Return meatballs to pan; simmer, uncovered, for about 10 minutes or until meatballs are cooked through. Season to taste.
**5** Serve meatballs with sour cream, coriander and, if you like, guacamole (see page 70).

**serving suggestion**
Serve with flour tortillas to scoop up the sauce.

# blackened steak salad

- 4 x 15cm (6-inch) flour tortillas
- 500g (1-pound) beef fillet
- ¼ teaspoon each dried oregano and thyme
- 2 teaspoons hot paprika
- 1 teaspoon ground black pepper
- ½ teaspoon cayenne pepper
- 3 medium tomatoes (450g), chopped finely
- 1 large green capsicum (bell pepper) (350g), chopped finely
- 1 lebanese cucumber (130g), seeded, chopped finely
- ½ cup coarsely chopped fresh mint
- 1 tablespoon olive oil
- 1 tablespoon balsamic vinegar
- 1 clove garlic, crushed
- lime wedges, to serve

**1** Cook tortillas on a heated oiled grill plate (or grill or barbecue) until browned lightly both sides. Break into coarse pieces.

**2** Rub beef with combined herbs and spices, season; cook on heated oiled grill plate (or grill or barbecue), turning, until browned and cooked as desired. Cover beef; stand for 5 minutes then slice thinly.

**3** Place beef and tortillas pieces in a large bowl with remaining ingredients; toss gently to combine, season to taste. Serve with lime wedges.

**serves** 4
**prep + cook time** 30 minutes
**nutritional count per serving** 13.7g total fat (4g saturated fat); 1304kJ (312 cal); 14.5g carbohydrate; 30.6g protein; 3.4g fibre

# chilli con carne

- 1 cup (200g) dried kidney beans
- 1.5kg (3 pounds) beef chuck steak
- 2 litres (8 cups) water
- 1 tablespoon olive oil
- 2 medium brown onions (300g), chopped coarsely
- 2 cloves garlic, crushed
- 2 teaspoons each ground coriander, cumin and sweet paprika
- ½ teaspoon cayenne pepper
- 800g (1½ pounds) canned crushed tomatoes
- 2 tablespoons tomato paste
- 4 green onions (scallions), chopped coarsely
- 2 tablespoons coarsely chopped fresh coriander (cilantro)
- ⅓ cup (65g) finely chopped pickled jalapeño chillies

**1** Place beans in a medium bowl, cover with water; stand overnight. Drain.

**2** Place beef and the water in a large saucepan; bring to the boil. Reduce heat; simmer, covered, 1½ hours.

**3** Drain beef in a large muslin-lined strainer over a large heatproof bowl; reserve 3½ cups of the cooking liquid. Using two forks, shred beef.

**4** Heat oil in same pan over medium heat; cook brown onion and garlic, stirring, about 5 minutes or until onion softens. Add spices; cook, stirring, 30 seconds or until fragrant. Add beans, tomatoes, paste and 2 cups of the reserved cooking liquid; bring to the boil. Reduce heat; simmer, covered, 1 hour.

**5** Add beef and remaining reserved cooking liquid to pan; simmer, covered, about 30 minutes or until beans are tender. Remove from heat; stir in green onions, coriander and chilli. Season to taste.

### serving suggestion

Serve with steamed rice; top with thinly sliced white onion and fresh coriander leaves (cilantro).

**serves** 8
**prep + cook time** 3½ hours (+ standing)
**nutritional count per serving** 11.5g total fat (4g saturated fat); 1513kJ (362 cal); 15.1g carbohydrate; 45.4g protein; 7.8g fibre

# corn and goat's cheese quesadillas

- 2 corn cobs (800g), trimmed
- 240g (7½ ounces) soft goat's cheese
- 8 x 20cm (8-inch) flour tortillas
- ½ cup (100g) drained char-grilled red capsicum (bell pepper), sliced thinly
- 2 tablespoons pickled sliced jalapeño chillies, drained
- ⅓ cup coarsely chopped fresh coriander (cilantro)
- 20g (¾ ounce) butter
- 40g (1½ ounces) baby spinach leaves
- lime wedges, to serve

**1** Cook corn on heated oiled grill plate (or grill or barbecue) until browned lightly and tender; when cool enough to handle, cut kernels from cobs.
**2** Spread cheese over tortillas. Top four of the tortillas with corn, capsicum, chilli and coriander, season; top with remaining tortillas. Press around edges firmly to seal quesadillas.
**3** Melt butter in a medium frying pan over medium heat; cook quesadillas, one at a time, until browned both sides and heated through.
**4** Serve quesadillas with spinach and lime wedges.

**tips** Tortillas are round, thin unleavened flat breads originating in Mexico. There are two types available, one made from wheat flour and the other from corn (maize meal). Mexican tortillas are very different from Spanish tortillas, which refer to an omelette, often consisting of eggs and potatoes.

**serves** 4
**prep + cook time** 30 minutes
**nutritional count per serving**
21.7g total fat
(10g saturated fat); 2169kJ
(519 cal); 57g carbohydrate;
19.8g protein; 8.6g fibre

**tip** Pasilla (pah-SEE-yah) chillies, also called 'chile negro' because of their dark brown colour, are the wrinkled, dried version of fresh chilaca chillies. About 20cm (8 inches) in length, a pasilla is only mildly hot, but possesses a rich flavour that adds a smoky depth to the overall recipe.

**serves** 4
**prep + cook time** 1¾ hours (+ standing)
**nutritional count per serving** 49.8g total fat

# spiced grilled beef with chilli beans

- 2 cups (400g) dried black beans
- 2 pasilla chillies (10g)
- ¼ cup (60ml) boiling water
- 2 tablespoons olive oil
- 1 medium brown onion (150g), chopped finely
- 3 cloves garlic, crushed
- ¼ cup (70g) tomato paste
- 4 medium tomatoes (600g), chopped coarsely
- ½ cup (125ml) water
- 2 tablespoons lime juice
- 2 tablespoons brown sugar
- 1 tablespoon dried marjoram
- 2 teaspoons smoked paprika
- 1kg (2 pounds) beef rump steak
- 8 x 20cm (8-inch) flour tortillas
- 1 small red onion (100g), sliced thinly
- 1 small iceberg lettuce, trimmed, shredded finely
- ⅓ cup firmly packed fresh coriander leaves (cilantro)
- ⅔ cup (160g) sour cream

**1** Place beans in a medium bowl, cover with water; stand overnight, drain.

**2** Cook beans in a large saucepan of boiling water, uncovered, until tender; drain. Rinse under cold water; drain.

**3** Meanwhile, cover chillies with the boiling water in small heatproof bowl; stand 20 minutes. Discard stalks from chillies. Blend or process chillies with soaking liquid until mixture is smooth.

**4** Heat half the oil in a large saucepan over high heat; cook brown onion and garlic, stirring, about 3 minutes or until onion softens. Add chilli mixture, paste, tomato, the water, juice and sugar; bring to the boil. Remove from heat; blend or process mixture until smooth.

**5** Return chilli mixture to pan; add beans, simmer, covered, 20 minutes. Uncover; simmer about 10 minutes or until sauce thickens. Season to taste.

**6** Meanwhile, combine marjoram, paprika and remaining oil in a large bowl; add beef, turn to coat in mixture, season. Cook beef on a heated oiled grill plate (or grill or barbecue) until browned both sides and cooked as desired. Cover beef; stand 10 minutes then slice thinly.

**7** Meanwhile, heat tortillas according to directions on packet. Serve tortillas topped with chilli beans, red onion, lettuce, beef, coriander and sour cream.

# chilli lamb roasts with black bean salad

- 1 cup (200g) dried black beans
- 2 mini lamb roasts (700g)
- ¼ cup (60ml) olive oil
- 1 large brown onion (200g), chopped finely
- 1 clove garlic, crushed
- 1 fresh long green chilli, chopped finely
- 1 teaspoon ground cumin
- 2 tablespoons red wine vinegar
- 1 large tomato (220g), seeded, chopped coarsely
- ½ cup firmly packed fresh coriander leaves (cilantro)
- 3 green onions (scallions), sliced thinly
- 2 tablespoons lime juice

## chilli marinade

- 3 fresh long green chillies, chopped finely
- 3 green onions (scallions), chopped finely
- 2 cloves garlic, crushed
- 1 teaspoon each ground allspice and dried thyme
- 1 teaspoon white (granulated) sugar
- 1 tablespoon worcestershire sauce
- 1 tablespoon lime juice

**1** Place beans in a medium bowl, cover with water; stand overnight.

**2** Combine ingredients for chilli marinade in a large bowl; add lamb, rub all over with marinade. Cover; refrigerate overnight.

**3** Preheat oven to 180°C/350°F.

**4** Drain beans; rinse under cold water. Cook beans in a medium saucepan of boiling water, uncovered, about 20 minutes or until tender; drain.

**5** Meanwhile, heat half the oil in a medium flameproof casserole dish over high heat on stove top; cook lamb until browned all over. Transfer to oven; roast lamb, uncovered, for about 20 minutes or until cooked as desired. Cover lamb; stand 10 minutes then slice thickly.

**6** Meanwhile, heat remaining oil in a medium saucepan over medium heat; cook brown onion, garlic, chilli and cumin, stirring, about 5 minutes or until onion softens. Add vinegar; cook, stirring, until liquid evaporates. Remove from heat.

**7** Combine onion mixture, beans, tomato, coriander, green onion and juice in a large bowl; season to taste.

**8** Serve lamb with salad.

**serves** 4
**prep + cook time** 1½ hours (+ standing & refrigeration)
**nutritional count per serving** 30.2g total fat (9g saturated fat); 2353kJ (563 cal); 22.4g carbohydrate; 49.8g protein; 12.8g fibre

**tip** Cook the onion mixture in the same saucepan that the beans are boiled in to save on the washing up.

**serves** 4
**prep + cook time**
45 minutes
**nutritional count per serving** 37.5g total fat (10.4g saturated fat); 3227kJ (772 cal); 62.3g carbohydrate; 45.8g protein; 8.4g fibre

# lamb fajitas

- 600g (1¼ pounds) lamb strips
- 3 cloves garlic, crushed
- ¼ cup (60ml) lemon juice
- 2 teaspoons ground cumin
- 1 tablespoon olive oil
- 1 large red capsicum (bell pepper) (350g), sliced thickly
- 1 large green capsicum (bell pepper) (350g), sliced thickly
- 1 medium yellow capsicum (bell pepper) (200g), sliced thickly
- 1 large red onion (300g), sliced thickly
- 8 x 20cm (8-inch) flour tortillas

guacamole

- 1 large avocado (320g), chopped coarsely
- ¼ cup finely chopped fresh coriander (cilantro)
- 1 tablespoon lime juice
- 1 small white onion (80g), chopped finely

salsa cruda

- 2 medium tomatoes (300g), seeded, chopped finely
- 1 fresh long green chilli, chopped finely
- ½ cup coarsely chopped fresh coriander (cilantro)
- 1 clove garlic, crushed
- 1 small white onion (80g), chopped finely
- 2 tablespoons lime juice

1 Combine lamb, garlic, juice, cumin and oil in large bowl. Cover; refrigerate.
2 Make guacamole.
3 Make salsa cruda.
4 Cook lamb, in batches, in a heated oiled frying pan over high heat, stirring, until browned all over and cooked as desired. Remove from pan. Cover to keep warm.
5 Cook capsicums and onion, in batches, in same pan over medium heat, stirring, until just softened. Remove mixture from pan.
6 Meanwhile, heat tortillas according to directions on packet.
7 Return lamb and capsicum mixture to pan; stir gently over medium heat until hot.
8 Serve lamb mixture with tortillas, guacamole and salsa cruda.

guacamole Combine ingredients in a small bowl; season to taste.

salsa cruda Combine ingredients in a small bowl; season to taste.

# black bean, corn and chipotle stew

- 1½ cups (300g) dried black beans
- 2 chipotle chillies
- ½ cup (125ml) boiling water
- 1 tablespoon cumin seeds
- 2 corn cobs (800g), trimmed
- 2 teaspoons olive oil
- 1 large brown onion (200g), chopped finely
- 800g (1½ pounds) canned crushed tomatoes
- 8 x 15cm (6-inch) white corn tortillas

## salsa fresca

- 1 small red onion (100g), chopped coarsely
- 1 small tomato (90g), chopped coarsely
- ½ cup coarsely chopped fresh coriander (cilantro)
- 1 lebanese cucumber (130g), chopped coarsely
- 1 tablespoon olive oil
- 2 tablespoons lemon juice

**1** Place beans in a medium bowl, cover with water; stand overnight, drain. Rinse under cold water; drain.

**2** Cook beans in a medium saucepan of boiling water for about 15 minutes or until beans are just tender. Drain.

**3** Preheat oven to 200°C/400°F.

**4** Cover chillies with the boiling water in a small heatproof bowl; stand 20 minutes. Discard stems; blend or process chilli and soaking liquid until smooth.

**5** Dry-fry cumin seeds in a small frying pan, stirring, until fragrant.

**6** Cook corn on a heated oiled grill plate (or grill or barbecue) until browned lightly and just tender. When cool enough to handle, cut corn kernels from cobs.

**7** Heat oil in a large flameproof dish over medium heat; cook onion, stirring, about 5 minutes or until softened. Add drained beans, chilli mixture, cumin seeds, tomatoes and half the corn; bring to the boil. Transfer to oven; bake, uncovered, for 20 minutes or until sauce thickens. Season to taste.

**8** Meanwhile, heat tortillas according to directions on packet. Make salsa fresca.

**9** Serve stew with tortillas and salsa.

salsa fresca Combine remaining corn with salsa ingredients in a medium bowl; season to taste.

**serves** 4
**prep + cook time**
1¼ hours (+ standing)
**nutritional count per serving** 10.4g total fat (1.3g saturated fat); 1839kJ (440 cal); 61.3g carbohydrate; 26.2g protein; 19.5g fibre

**tip** To add extra heat, serve some pickled sliced jalapeño chillies with the tacos.

# spicy chicken tacos

- 1 tablespoon olive oil
- 1 medium brown onion (150g), chopped finely
- 500g (1 pound) minced (ground) chicken
- 35g (1 ounce) packet taco seasoning mix
- 375g (12 ounces) bottled thick and chunky taco sauce
- ½ cup (125ml) water
- 10 stand 'n' stuff taco shells (140g)
- 1 cup (60g) finely shredded iceberg lettuce
- 1 medium carrot (120g), grated coarsely
- 125g (4 ounces) cherry tomatoes, quartered
- ½ cup (60g) coarsely grated cheddar
- ½ cup loosely packed fresh coriander leaves (cilantro)
- ⅓ cup (80g) sour cream

**1** Heat oil in a large frying pan over high heat; cook onion, stirring, until softened. Add chicken; cook, stirring, until browned. Add seasoning mix; cook, stirring, until fragrant. Add half the taco sauce and the water; cook over medium heat, stirring occasionally, for about 7 minutes or until mixture thickens. Remove from heat; season to taste.

**2** Meanwhile, heat taco shells according to directions on packet.

**3** Place chicken mixture into taco shells; top with lettuce, carrot, tomato, cheese, coriander, sour cream and remaining taco sauce.

**makes** 10
**prep + cook time** 25 minutes
**nutritional count per taco** 35.9g total fat (13.3g saturated fat); 2445kJ (585 cal); 29.7g carbohydrate; 33.2g protein; 6.7g fibre

# snapper Veracruz

- ¼ cup (60ml) light olive oil
- 2 medium green capsicums (bell peppers) (400g), chopped coarsely
- 1 medium brown onion (150g), chopped coarsely
- 2 fresh small red thai (serrano) chillies, chopped finely
- 2 cloves garlic, crushed
- ¼ teaspoon ground white pepper
- 1 teaspoon ground cinnamon
- 4 medium tomatoes (600g), chopped coarsely
- ¾ cup (110g) pimiento-stuffed green olives, chopped coarsely
- 2 tablespoons rinsed, drained capers, chopped coarsely
- 1 tablespoon lemon juice
- 2 x 800g (1½-pound) whole snapper
- lemon wedges, to serve

**1** Heat oil in a large frying pan over medium heat; cook capsicum, onion, chilli and garlic, stirring, about 5 minutes or until onion softens.

**2** Add pepper, cinnamon and tomato; simmer, uncovered, stirring occasionally, about 10 minutes or until tomatoes have broken down and sauce is thick. Stir in olives, capers and juice; season. Cool.

**3** Preheat oven to 180°C/350°F.

**4** Score fish three times on each side through the thickest part of the flesh; place fish in a large baking dish, season. Pour tomato mixture over fish.

**5** Bake fish, uncovered, about 30 minutes or until fish is cooked through. Serve with lemon wedges.

**serves** 4
**prep + cook time** 1 hour
**nutritional count per serving** 19.7g total fat (3.5g saturated fat); 1710kJ (409 cal); 8.1g carbohydrate; 46.7g protein; 5.5g fibre

**tip** This recipe is named after the large port city of Veracruz, where seafood is a specialty.

**tips** You can use olive oil instead of the walnut oil, if you prefer. Replace capsicums with store-bought char-grilled capsicums to save time.

**serves 6**
**prep + cook time**
1 hour (+ refrigeration)
**nutritional count per serving** 51.8g total fat (10.6g saturated fat); 3210kJ (768 cal); 51.9g carbohydrate; 21.2g protein; 7.1g fibre

# parmesan polenta with walnut capsicum salsa

- 20g (¾ ounce) butter
- 2 medium brown onions (300g), sliced thinly
- 1 tablespoon brown sugar
- 1 litre (4 cups) water
- 1⅓ cups (225g) polenta
- 2 teaspoons smoked paprika
- 1 tablespoon red wine vinegar
- 1 cup (80g) coarsely grated parmesan

## walnut capsicum salsa

- 2 large red capsicums (bell peppers) (700g)
- 1½ cups (150g) roasted walnuts, chopped coarsely
- 1 tablespoon red wine vinegar
- ¼ cup (60ml) walnut oil
- 1 clove garlic, crushed
- ½ cup coarsely chopped fresh flat-leaf parsley
- ⅓ cup coarsely chopped fresh coriander (cilantro)

**1** Melt butter in a medium frying pan over medium heat; cook onion, stirring, about 5 minutes or until softened. Add sugar and 2 tablespoons of the water; cook, stirring, about 5 minutes or until onion caramelises. Cover to keep warm.

**2** Oil a deep 22cm (9-inch) round cake pan. Bring remaining water to the boil in a medium saucepan. Gradually add polenta and paprika, stirring constantly. Simmer, stirring, about 8 minutes or until polenta thickens. Stir in vinegar and cheese.

**3** Spread half the polenta into pan. Spread onion mixture over polenta, then spread remaining polenta over onion. Cover; refrigerate until firm.

**4** Meanwhile, make walnut capsicum salsa.

**5** Turn polenta onto a board; cut into six wedges. Cook polenta, both sides, on a heated oiled grill plate (or grill or barbecue) until browned lightly and hot. Serve polenta with salsa.

### walnut capsicum salsa

Preheat grill (broiler). Quarter capsicums, discard seeds and membranes. Place capsicum, skin-side up, on an oven tray; grill until skin blisters and blackens. Cover capsicum pieces with plastic or paper for 5 minutes, peel away skin, then chop flesh coarsely. Combine capsicum and remaining ingredients in a small bowl; season.

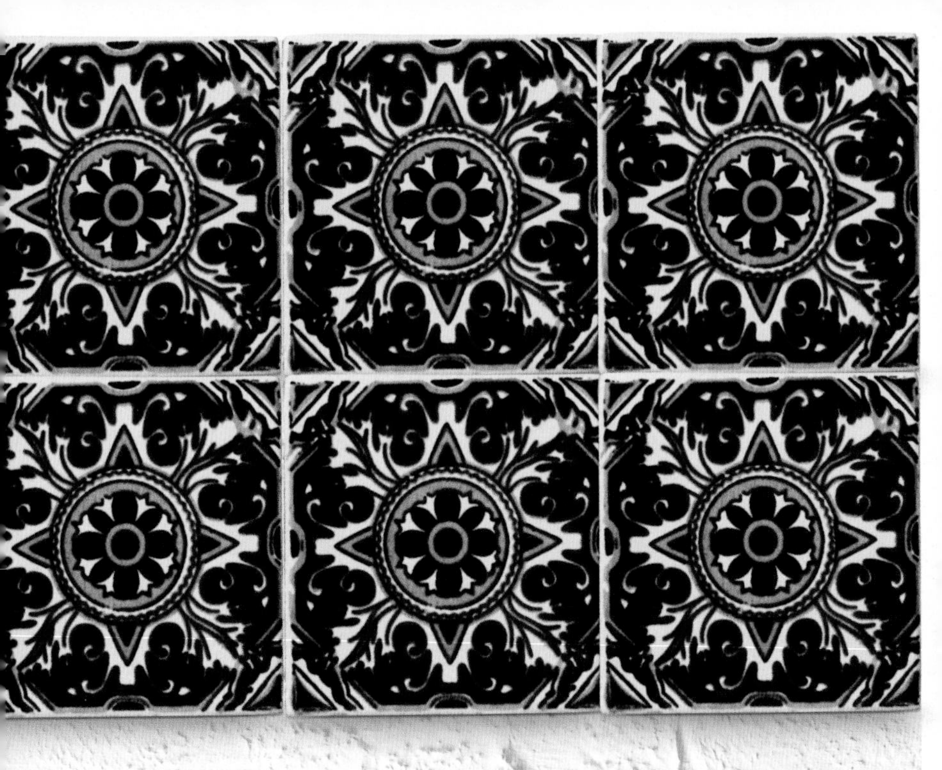

# sides & salsa

These sides and salsas will be fine accompaniments to any of the main meals in this book. Beans and rice feature extensively, but our favourites are the fresh flavours of the salsas.

# saffron rice with zucchini flowers

**You need to cook 1½ cups of white long-grain rice for this recipe. Spread the cooked rice on a flat tray and refrigerate, uncovered, overnight.**

- **12 zucchini flowers, stem attached (240g)**
- **45g (1½ ounces) butter**
- **1 large red onion (300g), cut into wedges**
- **2 teaspoons caraway seeds**
- **1 clove garlic, crushed**
- **4 cups (850g) cooked white long-grain rice**
- **1 teaspoon ground turmeric**
- **pinch saffron threads**
- **¼ cup (20g) flaked almonds, roasted**

**serves** 4
**prep + cook time** 30 minutes
**nutritional count per serving** 12.9g total fat (6.2g saturated fat); 1747kJ (418 cal); 65.3g carbohydrate; 8g protein; 3.6g fibre

**1** Remove flowers from zucchini; discard stamens from flowers. Slice zucchini thinly.
**2** Melt butter in a large frying pan over medium heat; cook onion, seeds and garlic, stirring, about 5 minutes or until onion softens. Add sliced zucchini; cook, stirring, until tender. Add rice, spices and zucchini flowers; cook, stirring, until hot. Stir in half the nuts; season to taste.
**3** Serve sprinkled with remaining nuts.

**tip** Zucchini is also known as courgette. The 'stem' is the baby zucchini attached to the flower; when harvested young, its edible flowers can be stuffed then either deep-fried or oven-baked to make a delicious appetiser.

# mexican rice

- 1 medium brown onion (150g), quartered
- 2 large tomatoes (440g), quartered
- 2 cloves garlic, unpeeled
- 2 tablespoons olive oil
- ½ teaspoon chilli powder
- 1½ cups (300g) white long-grain rice
- 2 cups (500ml) chicken stock
- 1 small carrot (70g), sliced thinly
- ½ cup (60g) frozen peas
- 125g (4 ounces) canned corn kernels, rinsed, drained
- ⅓ cup coarsely chopped fresh coriander (cilantro)

**1** Preheat oven to 200°C/400°F.

**2** Place onion, tomato and garlic on an oiled oven tray; drizzle with half the oil. Roast, uncovered, about 25 minutes or until vegetables soften. When cool enough to handle, peel tomato and garlic.

**3** Blend or process onion, tomato, garlic and chilli powder until smooth (you need 2 cups puree).

**4** Heat remaining oil in a medium saucepan over medium heat; cook rice, stirring, 3 minutes. Add tomato mixture; cook, stirring, about 8 minutes or until almost all of the liquid is evaporated.

**5** Add stock, carrot, peas and corn to pan; bring to the boil. Reduce heat; simmer, covered, over low heat, about 10 minutes or until rice is tender and liquid is absorbed. Remove from heat; stand, covered, 10 minutes. Fluff rice with a fork; season to taste. Serve sprinkled with coriander.

**serves** 4
**prep + cook time** 1 hour
**nutritional count per serving** 7.9g total fat (1.2g saturated fat); 1739kJ (416 cal); 72.9g carbohydrate; 10g protein; 5.3g fibre

- 1 medium mango (430g), chopped coarsely
- 1 large avocado (320g), chopped coarsely
- 1 small red onion (100g), chopped finely
- 1 small red capsicum (bell pepper) (150g), chopped finely
- 1 fresh small red thai (serrano) chilli, chopped finely
- 2 tablespoons lime juice

1 Combine ingredients in a medium bowl; season to taste.

serving suggestion Serve with roasted corn, grilled chicken or salmon fillets.

# mango and avocado salsa

**makes** 2½ cups
**prep time** 15 minutes
**nutritional count per tablespoon** 1.7g total fat (0.4g saturated fat); 100kJ (24 cal); 1.6g carbohydrate; 0.4g protein; 0.4g fibre

serves 4
**prep + cook time** 2 hours (+ standing)
**nutritional count per serving** 4.8g total fat (1.5g saturated fat); 1267kJ (303 cal); 32.1g carbohydrate; 21.6g protein; 12.8g fibre

# drunken beans

- **1 cup (200g) dried pinto beans**
- **3 rindless bacon slices (195g), chopped coarsely**
- **1 medium brown onion (150g), chopped finely**
- **1 clove garlic, crushed**
- **1 teaspoon ground cumin**
- **½ teaspoon cayenne pepper**
- **1 tablespoon tomato paste**
- **400g (12½ ounces) canned crushed tomatoes**
- **1 cup (250ml) water**
- **1 cup (250ml) beer**
- **1 tablespoon worcestershire sauce**
- **2 tablespoons brown sugar**

**1** Place beans in a medium bowl, cover with water; stand overnight. Drain.

**2** Cook bacon, onion, garlic and spices in a oiled large saucepan over high heat, stirring, about 3 minutes or until onion softens.

**3** Add drained beans and remaining ingredients to pan; bring to the boil. Reduce heat; simmer, covered, about 1½ hours or until beans are just tender. Season to taste.

# refried beans

- **1¾ cups (350g) dried kidney beans**
- **1.5 litres (6 cups) water**
- **1 small brown onion (80g), chopped coarsely**
- **1 clove garlic, crushed**
- **1 dried bay leaf**
- **½ fresh small green chilli, chopped finely**
- **2 tablespoons olive oil**
- **1 small brown onion (80g), chopped finely**
- **1 large tomato (220g), peeled, chopped finely**

**1** Place beans in a medium bowl, cover with water; stand overnight. Drain.
**2** Combine beans, the water, coarsely chopped onion, garlic, bay leaf and chilli in a large saucepan; bring to the boil. Reduce heat; simmer, covered, about 1 hour or until beans are tender.
**3** Drain bean mixture over a heatproof bowl; discard bay leaf; reserve ½ cup cooking liquid. Blend or process bean mixture with reserved cooking liquid until coarsely mashed.
**4** Heat oil in a large frying pan over medium heat; cook finely chopped onion, stirring, about 5 minutes or until onion softens. Add tomato; cook, stirring, until tomato softens. Stir in bean mixture; cook over low heat, stirring, about 10 minutes or until thickened; season.

**serving suggestions**
Serve as a dip with corn chips or use as a vegetarian filling for tacos, quesadillas or burritos.

**serves** 6
**prep + cook time** 2½ hours
**nutritional count per serving** 7.2g total fat (1g saturated fat); 1003kJ (240 cal); 23g carbohydrate; 13.9g protein; 13.4g fibre

**serves** 4
**prep + cook time** 1 hour
**nutritional count per serving** 3.3g total fat (1g saturated fat); 2215kJ (530 cal); 99.3g carbohydrate; 20.8g protein; 7.1g fibre

# red beans and rice

**You need one trimmed corn cob to get the amount of corn kernels required; you can use the same amount of drained canned corn kernels or frozen corn kernels, if you prefer.**

- **2 rindless bacon slices (130g), chopped coarsely**
- **1 medium brown onion (150g), chopped finely**
- **2 cloves garlic, crushed**
- **1 small red capsicum (bell pepper) (150g), chopped finely**
- **1 tablespoon tomato paste**
- **1 tablespoon red wine vinegar**
- **1 teaspoon smoked paprika**
- **2 cups (400g) white long-grain rice**
- **1 dried bay leaf**
- **1 cup (250ml) chicken stock**
- **2¼ cups (560ml) water**
- **410g (13 ounces) canned kidney beans, rinsed, drained**
- **½ cup (80g) corn kernels**
- **1 tablespoon lime juice**

**1** Cook bacon in a heated large frying pan over high heat, stirring, until starting to crisp. Add onion, garlic and capsicum; cook, stirring, about 3 minutes or until onion softens.
**2** Add paste, vinegar and paprika; cook, stirring, 1 minute. Add rice; cook, stirring, 2 minutes.
**3** Add bay leaf, stock, the water and beans; bring to the boil. Reduce heat; simmer, covered, 20 minutes. Add corn; cook, covered, about 5 minutes or until rice is tender. Remove from heat; stand, covered, 5 minutes. Stir in juice; season to taste.

**serving suggestion**
Serve with grilled chicken, or to accompany many of the main meals in this book.

**tips** Capsicum, or bell pepper, are native to Central and South America. Capsicums come in several colours – red, green, yellow, orange or purplish black – each of which has an individual flavour. Discard the seeds and membranes before using.

- 2 medium avocados (500g)
- ½ small red onion (50g), chopped finely
- 1 medium roma (egg) tomato (75g), seeded, chopped finely
- 1 tablespoon lime juice
- ¼ cup coarsely chopped fresh coriander (cilantro)

1 Mash avocados in a medium bowl; stir in remaining ingredients. Season to taste.

**serving suggestion** Serve as a dip with corn chips; it also goes well with nachos, burritos and fajitas.

# guacamole

**makes** 2½ cups
**prep time** 10 minutes
**nutritional count per tablespoon** 2.6g total fat (0.6g saturated fat); 109kJ (26 cal); 0.2g carbohydrate; 0.3g protein; 0.2g fibre

**serves** 6
**prep + cook time** 1¾ hours (+ standing)
**nutritional count per serving** 9.9g total fat (1.5g saturated fat); 790kJ (189 cal); 9.7g carbohydrate; 11.6g protein; 7.8g fibre

# black bean and mango salsa

- 1 cup (200g) dried black beans
- 1 lebanese cucumber (130g), seeded, sliced thinly
- 1 medium mango (430g), chopped finely
- 1 cup loosely packed fresh coriander leaves (cilantro)

## sweet chilli dressing

- 1 tablespoon olive oil
- 1 tablespoon sweet chilli sauce
- 1 tablespoon lime juice

**1** Place beans in a medium bowl, cover with water; stand overnight. Drain.
**2** Cook beans in a medium saucepan of boiling water until tender; drain.
**3** Meanwhile, make sweet chilli dressing.
**4** Place beans in a medium bowl with dressing and remaining ingredients; toss gently to combine, season to taste.

**sweet chilli dressing** Combine ingredients in a small bowl.

# grilled corn and zucchini salsa

- 2 corn cobs (800g), trimmed
- 100g (3 ounces) baby zucchini, halved lengthways
- 2 large avocados (640g), chopped coarsely
- 200g (6½ ounces) grape tomatoes, halved
- 1 medium red onion (170g), sliced thickly
- ¼ cup coarsely chopped fresh coriander (cilantro)
- 1 tablespoon sweet chilli sauce
- ⅓ cup (80ml) lime juice
- 2 fresh small red thai (serrano) chillies, sliced thinly

**makes** 7 cups
**prep + cook time** 30 minutes
**nutritional count per tablespoon** 1.3g total fat (0.3g saturated fat); 84kJ (20 cal); 1.4g carbohydrate; 0.5g protein; 0.5g fibre

**1** Cook corn and zucchini on a heated oiled grill plate (or grill or barbecue) until tender and browned lightly. When cool enough to handle, cut kernels from cobs.

**2** Place corn and zucchini in a large bowl with avocado, tomato, onion and coriander. Add combined sauce, juice and chilli; toss gently to combine. Season to taste.

**serving suggestion**
Serve with grilled salmon or chicken, barbecued beef rump steak, or chicken or beef fajitas. This recipe makes enough for six servings.

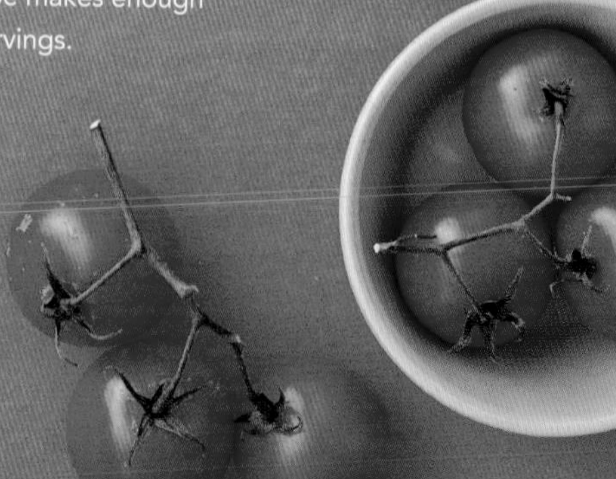

**BEANS**

**black** also known as turtle beans; a common ingredient in Caribbean and Latin American soups, salsas and salads. They are not the same as chinese black beans, which are fermented soya beans. Available from greengrocers and delicatessens.

**kidney** medium-size red bean, slightly floury in texture yet sweet in flavour; it's found in bean mixes and is the bean used in chilli con carne.

**mexican-style** are a mildly spiced canned combination of kidney or pinto beans, capsicum and tomato.

**BEEF**

**chuck steak** comes from the neck and shoulder of the beef, and tends to be chewy but flavourful and inexpensive. A good cut for stewing.

**fillet** cut from beef tenderloin.

**rump steak** tender boneless cut taken from the upper part of the round (hindquarter).

**BUTTER** 125g is equal to one stick (4 ounces) of butter.

**BUTTERMILK** originally the term given to the slightly sour liquid left after butter was churned from cream, today it is made similarly to yogurt. Sold alongside all fresh milk products in supermarkets; despite the implication of its name, it is low in fat.

**CAPERS** the grey-green buds of a warm climate (usually Mediterranean) shrub, sold either dried and salted or pickled in a vinegar brine.

**baby capers** those picked early, are very small, fuller-flavoured and more expensive than the full-size one. All capers must be rinsed well before using.

**CAPSICUM** also known as bell pepper or, simply, pepper. Be sure to discard seeds and membranes before use.

**char-grilled** available loose from delis or packed in jars in oil or brine.

**CARAWAY SEEDS** a member of the parsley family; is available in seed or ground form. Has a pungent aroma and a distinctly sweet but tangy flavour.

**CAYENNE PEPPER** a long, thin-fleshed, extremely hot red chilli; usually purchased dried and ground.

**CHEESE**

**cream** commonly known as Philadelphia or Philly, a soft cow's-milk cheese. Also available as spreadable light cream cheese, a light version of Philadelphia; is a blend of cottage and cream cheeses.

**goat's** made from goats' milk; has an earthy, strong taste. Available in both soft and firm textures, in various shapes and sizes, sometimes rolled in ash or herbs.

**parmesan** a hard, grainy cow's-milk cheese. The curd is salted in brine for a month before being aged for up to 2 years in humid conditions.

**CHICKEN**

**drumstick** leg with skin and bone intact.

**small chickens** (spatchcock) a small chicken (poussin), no more than 6 weeks old, weighing a maximum 500g.

**thigh cutlet** thigh with skin and centre bone intact; sometimes found skinned with bone intact.

**CHILLI** available in many types and sizes. Use rubber gloves when seeding and chopping fresh chillies as they can burn your skin. Removing seeds and membranes lessens the heat level.

**jalapeño** fairly hot green chillies, available bottled in brine or fresh from specialty greengrocers.

**chipotle** are what fresh jalapeño chillies are called after they've been dried and smoked. Having a deep, intensely smoky flavour rather than a searing heat, chipotles are dark brown, almost black in appearance; available from specialty spice stores and gourmet delicatessens.

**long red** available both fresh and dried; a generic term used for any moderately hot, long thin chilli.

**pasilla** or chile negro, is a long dried chilli named for its dark wrinkled skin. It turns from dark green to dark brown when fully mature.

**powder** the Asian variety, made from dried ground thai chillies, is the hottest; it can be used as a substitute for fresh chillies – ½ teaspoon ground chilli powder to 1 medium chopped fresh chilli.

# glossary

**thai** bright red to dark green in colour, ranging in size from small to long and thin; among the hottest of chillies.

**CHORIZO SAUSAGE** a highly seasoned, coarsely ground pork sausage flavoured with garlic, chilli powder and other spices. It's widely used in both Mexican and Spanish cookery. Mexican chorizo is made with fresh pork, while the Spanish version uses smoked pork. Available both cured and raw.

**CORIANDER** also known as pak chee, cilantro or chinese parsley; bright-green leafy herb with a pungent flavour. Both the stems and roots of coriander are also used; wash under cold water, removing any dirt clinging to the roots; scrape the roots with a small flat knife to remove some of the outer fibrous skin. Don't substitute ground coriander for fresh as the tastes are completely different.

**CORN CHIPS** made from washed corn that is ground to produce a dough, and then rolled into a thin sheet and cut into the appropriate shapes. The dough is then toasted and fried until crisp.

**CREAM** we use fresh cream, also known as pouring cream and pure cream, unless otherwise stated. It has no additives, unlike commercially thickened cream. Minimum fat content 35%.

**sour** a thick commercially-cultured soured cream. Minimum fat content 35%.

**DRIED HERBS**

**marjoram** is similar in flavour to oregano, but is milder and sweeter in taste.

**oregano** a herb also known as wild marjoram; has a woody stalk with clumps of tiny, dark green leaves that have a pungent, peppery flavour. Used fresh and dried.

**thyme** a member of the mint family; there are many types of this herb but two that we use most – the 'household' variety, simply called thyme in most shops, is French thyme; it has tiny grey-green leaves that give off a pungent minty, light-lemon aroma.

**EGGS** some recipes in this book may call for raw or barely cooked eggs; exercise caution if there is a salmonella problem in your area.

**FLAT-LEAF PARSLEY** also known as continental parsley or italian parsley.

**FLOUR, PLAIN** (all-purpose) an general purpose flour made from wheat.

**LAMB MINI ROAST** is cut from the lean rump section of the lamb leg.

**LEBANESE CUCUMBER** short, slender and thin-skinned. Probably the most popular variety because of its tender, edible skin, tiny, yielding seeds, and sweet, fresh and flavoursome taste.

**LETTUCE**

**cos** also known as romaine; the traditional Caesar salad lettuce. Baby cos, having tiny leaves, is also available.

**iceberg** a heavy, firm round lettuce with tightly packed leaves and crisp texture.

**MINT** a herb that has many varieties and includes spearmint, common mint and peppermint. Spearmint has long, smooth leaves, and is the one that greengrocers sell, while common mint, with rounded, pebbly leaves, is the one that most people grow.

**OIL**

**walnut** pressed from ground walnuts.

**OLIVES, PIMIENTO-STUFFED GREEN** a green olive stuffed with a morsel of capsicum, which adds a flash of colour.

**ONION**

**brown and white** these are interchangeable, however, white onions have a more pungent flesh.

**green** also known as scallion or (incorrectly) shallot; an immature onion picked before the bulb has formed, having a long, bright-green edible stalk.

**red** also known as spanish, red spanish or bermuda onion; a sweet-flavoured, large, purple-red onion.

**OREGANO** see dried herbs.

**POLENTA** also known as cornmeal; a flour-like cereal made of dried corn (maize) sold ground in different textures; also the name of the dish made from it.

**PORK NECK** sometimes called pork scotch; a boneless cut from the foreloin.

SAUCE

**sweet chilli** a mild sauce made from red chillies, sugar, garlic and vinegar.

**Tabasco** the brand name of an extremely fiery sauce made from vinegar, red thai chillies and salt.

**tomato pasta** a blend of tomatoes, herbs and spices.

**worcestershire** a thin, spicy, dark-brown sauce made from garlic, soy sauce, tamarind, onions, molasses, anchovies, and vinegar.

SPICES

**allspice** also known as pimento or jamaican pepper; available whole or ground. Tastes like a blend of cinnamon, clove and nutmeg – all spices.

**cinnamon** the dried inner bark of the shoots of the cinnamon tree; available in stick (quill) or ground form. Cinnamon sticks must be removed before serving the dish.

**cloves** the dried flower buds of a tropical tree; can be used whole or in ground form. Has a distinctively pungent and 'spicy' scent and flavour.

**coriander** seeds and ground coriander must never be used to replace fresh coriander or vice versa, as the tastes are completely different.

**cumin** also known as zeera or comino; has a spicy, nutty flavour.

**nutmeg** the dried nut of an evergreen tree native to Indonesia; it is available in ground form or you can grate your own with a fine grater.

**paprika** a ground dried sweet red capsicum (bell pepper); there are many grades and types available, including sweet, hot, mild and smoked.

**turmeric** also known as kamin; known for the golden colour it imparts to the dishes of which it's a part.

**saffron threads** are available in strands or ground form; imparts a yellow-orange colour to food once infused. The quality varies greatly; the best is the most expensive spice in the world. Should be stored in the freezer.

**SPINACH** also known as english spinach and, incorrectly, silver beet. Its thick, soft oval leaves and green stems are both edible. Baby spinach is also available.

SUGAR

**brown** extremely soft, finely granulated sugar retaining molasses for its characteristic colour and flavour.

**white** a coarsely granulated table sugar, also known as crystal sugar.

TACO

**seasoning mix** found in most supermarkets; is meant to duplicate the taste of a Mexican sauce made from oregano, cumin, chillies and other spices.

**stand 'n' stuff shells** taco shells with a flat base, which keeps them standing upright.

TOMATO

**cherry** also known as tiny tim or tom thumb tomatoes, small and round.

**grape** so-named because they are about the size of a grape; they can be oblong, pear- or grape-shaped.

**roma** also called egg or plum tomato, these are smallish, oval-shaped tomatoes.

**TORTILLAS** this thin, round unleavened bread originated in Mexico. There are two types available, one made from wheat flour and the other from corn (maize meal).

VINEGAR

**balsamic** originally made from the juice of Trebbiano grapes from Modena, Italy; it is a deep rich brown colour with a sweet and sour flavour. There are now many balsamic vinegars on the market ranging in pungency and quality depending on how long they have been aged. Quality can be determined up to a point by price; use the most expensive sparingly.

**brown malt** made from fermented malt and beech shavings.

**cider** (apple cider) made from fermented apples.

**red wine** based on fermented red wine.

**sherry** made from a blend of wines and left in wood vats to mature where they develop a rich mellow flavour.

**WHITE FISH FILLETS** bream, blue eye, flathead, swordfish, ling, whiting, jewfish, snapper or sea perch are all good choices. Check for any small bones in the fillets and use tweezers to remove them.

# conversion chart

## measures

One Australian metric measuring cup holds approximately 250ml, one Australian metric tablespoon holds 20ml, one Australian metric teaspoon holds 5ml. The difference between one country's measuring cups and another's is within a 2- or 3-teaspoon variance, and will not affect your cooking results. North America, New Zealand and the United Kingdom use a 15ml tablespoon. All cup and spoon measurements are level. The most accurate way of measuring dry ingredients is to weigh them. When measuring liquids, use a clear glass or plastic jug with metric markings.

We use large eggs with an average weight of 60g.

## dry measures

| METRIC | IMPERIAL |
|---|---|
| 15g | ½oz |
| 30g | 1oz |
| 60g | 2oz |
| 90g | 3oz |
| 125g | 4oz (¼lb) |
| 155g | 5oz |
| 185g | 6oz |
| 220g | 7oz |
| 250g | 8oz (½lb) |
| 280g | 9oz |
| 315g | 10oz |
| 345g | 11oz |
| 375g | 12oz (¾lb) |
| 410g | 13oz |
| 440g | 14oz |
| 470g | 15oz |
| 500g | 16oz (1lb) |
| 750g | 24oz (1½lb) |
| 1kg | 32oz (2lb) |

## liquid measures

| METRIC | IMPERIAL |
|---|---|
| 30ml | 1 fluid oz |
| 60ml | 2 fluid oz |
| 100ml | 3 fluid oz |
| 125ml | 4 fluid oz |
| 150ml | 5 fluid oz |
| 190ml | 6 fluid oz |
| 250ml | 8 fluid oz |
| 300ml | 10 fluid oz |
| 500ml | 16 fluid oz |
| 600ml | 20 fluid oz |
| 1000ml (1 litre) | 1¾ pints |

## length measures

| METRIC | IMPERIAL |
|---|---|
| 3mm | ⅛in |
| 6mm | ¼in |
| 1cm | ½in |
| 2cm | ¾in |
| 2.5cm | 1in |
| 5cm | 2in |
| 6cm | 2½in |
| 8cm | 3in |
| 10cm | 4in |
| 13cm | 5in |
| 15cm | 6in |
| 18cm | 7in |
| 20cm | 8in |
| 23cm | 9in |
| 25cm | 10in |
| 28cm | 11in |
| 30cm | 12in (1ft) |

## oven temperatures

These oven temperatures are only a guide for conventional ovens. For fan-forced ovens, check the manufacturer's manual.

| | °C (CELSIUS) | °F (FAHRENHEIT) |
|---|---|---|
| Very slow | 120 | 250 |
| Slow | 150 | 275-300 |
| Moderately slow | 160 | 325 |
| Moderate | 180 | 350-375 |
| Moderately hot | 200 | 400 |
| Hot | 220 | 425-450 |
| Very hot | 240 | 475 |

The imperial measurements used in these recipes are approximate only. Do not mix measurements; use either all metric or all imperial. Measurements for cake pans are approximate only. Using same-shaped cake pans of a similar size should not affect the outcome of your baking. We measure the inside top of the cake pan to determine sizes.

# index

Published in 2013 by Bauer Media Books, Sydney
Bauer Media Books are published by Bauer Media Limited
54 Park St, Sydney
GPO Box 4088, Sydney, NSW 2001.
phone (02) 9282 8618; fax (02) 9126 3702
www.awwcookbooks.com.au

MEDIA GROUP

BAUER MEDIA BOOKS
Publisher - Sally Wright
Editorial & Food Director - Pamela Clark
Director of Sales, Marketing & Rights - Brian Cearnes
Creative Director - Hieu Chi Nguyen

Published and Distributed in the United Kingdom by Octopus Publishing Group
Endeavour House
189 Shaftesbury Avenue
London WC2H 8JY
United Kingdom
phone (+44)(0)207 632 5400; fax (+44)(0)207 632 5405
info@octopus-publishing.co.uk;
www.octopusbooks.co.uk

Printed by 1010 Printing, China

International foreign language rights, Brian Cearnes, Bauer Media Books
bcearnes@bauer-media.com.au

A catalogue record for this book is available from the British Library.
ISBN: 978-1-74245-383-5 (paperback)